50 South African Recipes for Home

By: Kelly Johnson

Table of Contents

- Bunny Chow
- Bobotie
- Malva Pudding
- Boerewors Rolls
- Sosaties
- Potjiekos
- Waterblommetjie Bredie
- Koeksisters
- Durban Chicken Curry
- Chakalaka
- Amarula Dom Pedro
- Pap en Wors
- Umngqusho
- Karoo Lamb Potjie
- Braaibroodjies
- Bredie
- Melktert
- Geelrys
- Boeber
- Koeksister Ice Cream Sandwich
- Samp and Beans
- Tomato Bredie
- Vetkoek with Mince
- Grilled Snoek
- Pickled Fish
- Cape Malay Chicken Curry
- Denningvleis
- Cape Malay Roti
- Potato and Pea Curry
- Cape Malay Pickled Fish
- Ostrich Bobotie
- Cape Malay Samoosas
- Amasi Chicken
- South African Milk Tart
- Tomato Smoor

- Cape Malay Snoek Pâté
- Cape Malay Tomato Bredie
- Amarula Malva Pudding
- Cape Malay Lamb Biryani
- Samp and Lamb Stew
- Rooibos-Infused Salmon
- Peppermint Crisp Tart
- Biltong and Cheese Quiche
- Koeksister Bread Pudding
- Peri-Peri Chicken
- Vetkoek with Avo and Biltong
- Cape Malay Hertzoggies
- Chutney Chicken
- Pumpkin Fritters
- Rooibos and Honey Glazed Chicken Wings

Bunny Chow

Ingredients:

For the Curry:

- 2 tablespoons vegetable oil
- 1 onion, finely chopped
- 2 tomatoes, chopped
- 2 teaspoons ginger-garlic paste
- 1 kg (2.2 lbs) chicken, lamb, or vegetables (cubed)
- 2 tablespoons curry powder
- 1 teaspoon ground cumin
- 1 teaspoon ground coriander
- 1 teaspoon turmeric
- 1 teaspoon chili powder (adjust to taste)
- Salt and pepper to taste
- Fresh coriander leaves for garnish

For the Bunny Chow:

- 4 small round or oblong bread loaves
- Butter (optional)

Instructions:

For the Curry:

Saute Aromatics:
- In a large pot, heat vegetable oil over medium heat. Add chopped onions and cook until softened.

Add Ginger-Garlic Paste:
- Add ginger-garlic paste to the onions and cook for another minute until fragrant.

Add Spices:
- Add curry powder, ground cumin, ground coriander, turmeric, and chili powder. Stir well to coat the onions in the spices.

Cook Tomatoes:
- Add chopped tomatoes and cook until they break down and form a thick, aromatic base.

Add Meat or Vegetables:

- Add the cubed chicken, lamb, or vegetables to the pot. Season with salt and pepper. Cook until the meat is browned or the vegetables are tender.

Simmer:
- Add water or chicken/vegetable broth to achieve the desired consistency. Simmer until the curry is cooked through and flavorful.

Garnish:
- Garnish with fresh coriander leaves and adjust the seasoning if necessary.

For the Bunny Chow:

Prepare Bread Loaves:
- Cut a rectangular portion from the top of each bread loaf and hollow it out, creating a bread "bowl." Optionally, brush the insides with butter.

Serve Curry:
- Ladle the prepared curry into each hollowed-out bread loaf.

Garnish:
- Garnish with additional coriander leaves.

Serve:
- Serve Bunny Chow immediately. The bread serves as both a vessel for the curry and a delicious accompaniment.

Enjoy this South African street food classic, Bunny Chow! It's a hearty and flavorful dish that's perfect for sharing.

Bobotie

Ingredients:

For the Bobotie:

- 1 kg (2.2 lbs) ground beef or lamb
- 2 slices white bread, crusts removed
- 1 cup milk
- 2 onions, finely chopped
- 2 tablespoons vegetable oil
- 2 cloves garlic, minced
- 1 tablespoon curry powder
- 1 teaspoon ground turmeric
- 1 teaspoon ground coriander
- 1 teaspoon ground cumin
- 1 teaspoon ground cinnamon
- 2 tablespoons apricot jam
- 2 tablespoons chutney
- 2 tablespoons vinegar
- Salt and black pepper to taste
- 1/2 cup raisins or sultanas
- 1/4 cup flaked almonds (optional)

For the Topping:

- 2 large eggs
- 1 cup milk
- Pinch of salt

For Serving:

- Cooked yellow rice
- Chutney or mango atchar

Instructions:

Preheat Oven:
- Preheat your oven to 180°C (350°F).

Prepare Bread Mixture:
- In a bowl, soak the bread slices in 1 cup of milk until softened. Mash it with a fork to form a smooth paste.

Cook Meat Mixture:
- In a large skillet, sauté the finely chopped onions in vegetable oil until softened. Add minced garlic and cook for an additional minute.
- Add the ground meat and brown it. Break up any clumps with a spoon.

Add Spices and Flavorings:
- Stir in curry powder, ground turmeric, ground coriander, ground cumin, and ground cinnamon. Mix well.
- Add apricot jam, chutney, vinegar, salt, and black pepper. Stir until combined.

Combine Bread Mixture:
- Add the bread and milk mixture to the meat mixture. Mix thoroughly.
- Fold in raisins or sultanas and flaked almonds if using.

Transfer to Baking Dish:
- Transfer the mixture to a greased baking dish, spreading it evenly.

Prepare Topping:
- In a separate bowl, beat eggs. Add milk and a pinch of salt. Mix well.

Top and Bake:
- Pour the egg mixture over the meat mixture in the baking dish.

Bake:
- Bake in the preheated oven for about 40-45 minutes or until the topping is set and golden brown.

Serve:
- Serve Bobotie hot with yellow rice and a side of chutney or mango atchar.

Enjoy this delicious and aromatic South African dish, Bobotie! It's a unique and flavorful addition to your culinary repertoire.

Malva Pudding

Ingredients:

For the Pudding:

- 1 cup all-purpose flour
- 1 teaspoon baking soda
- 1/2 teaspoon salt
- 1 cup granulated sugar
- 1 large egg
- 1 tablespoon apricot jam
- 1 tablespoon vinegar
- 1 cup milk

For the Sauce:

- 1 cup heavy cream
- 1 cup unsalted butter
- 1 cup sugar
- 1/2 cup hot water

Instructions:

Preheat Oven:
- Preheat your oven to 180°C (350°F).

Grease Baking Dish:
- Grease a medium-sized baking dish.

Prepare Dry Ingredients:
- In a bowl, sift together the flour, baking soda, and salt.

Beat Sugar and Egg:
- In a separate large bowl, beat the sugar and egg together until creamy.

Add Jam and Vinegar:
- Add the apricot jam and vinegar to the sugar and egg mixture. Mix well.

Combine Dry Ingredients:
- Gradually add the sifted dry ingredients to the wet ingredients, alternating with the milk. Mix until smooth.

Pour into Baking Dish:
- Pour the batter into the greased baking dish.

Bake:

- Bake in the preheated oven for approximately 45-50 minutes or until a skewer inserted into the center comes out clean.

Prepare Sauce:
- While the pudding is baking, prepare the sauce. In a saucepan, combine the heavy cream, butter, sugar, and hot water. Heat over low heat, stirring until the butter is melted and the sugar is dissolved.

Pour Sauce Over Pudding:
- As soon as the pudding is out of the oven, pour the hot sauce over it, allowing the pudding to absorb the liquid.

Let it Stand:
- Allow the Malva Pudding to stand for a few minutes, letting it soak up the sauce.

Serve:
- Serve the Malva Pudding warm, either on its own or with a scoop of vanilla ice cream or custard.

Enjoy the sweet and comforting indulgence of Malva Pudding, a delightful South African dessert!

Boerewors Rolls

Ingredients:

For the Boerewors:

- 500g boerewors (South African sausage)
- 2 tablespoons vegetable oil

For Serving:

- Soft rolls or baguettes
- Tomato sauce (ketchup)
- Mustard
- Onion rings
- Fresh coriander or parsley, chopped (optional)

Instructions:

Preheat Grill:
- Preheat your grill or braai (barbecue) to medium-high heat.

Grill Boerewors:
- Brush the boerewors with vegetable oil to prevent sticking on the grill.
- Grill the boerewors for about 15-20 minutes, turning occasionally until fully cooked and nicely browned.

Prepare Rolls:
- Slice the rolls or baguettes lengthwise, creating a pocket to hold the boerewors.

Assemble Boerewors Rolls:
- Place a grilled boerewors inside each roll.

Add Toppings:
- Drizzle tomato sauce and mustard over the boerewors.
- Add a few onion rings on top.

Garnish:
- Sprinkle with chopped fresh coriander or parsley if desired.

Serve:
- Serve the Boerewors Rolls immediately while hot.

Boerewors Rolls are often enjoyed as a quick and tasty snack during outdoor gatherings or events. Customize the toppings to your liking for an authentic South African experience!

Sosaties

Ingredients:

For the Marinade:

- 2 lbs (about 1 kg) lamb, cut into cubes
- 2 onions, finely chopped
- 1 cup apricot jam
- 1/2 cup white wine vinegar
- 1/2 cup vegetable oil
- 2 tablespoons curry powder
- 1 tablespoon ground coriander
- 1 teaspoon ground turmeric
- 1 teaspoon ground cumin
- Salt and pepper to taste

For the Skewers:

- Wooden skewers, soaked in water for at least 30 minutes

Instructions:

Prepare Marinade:
- In a large bowl, combine chopped onions, apricot jam, white wine vinegar, vegetable oil, curry powder, ground coriander, ground turmeric, ground cumin, salt, and pepper. Mix well to create the marinade.

Marinate Lamb:
- Add the lamb cubes to the marinade, making sure each piece is well coated. Cover the bowl and let it marinate for at least 2-4 hours, or preferably overnight in the refrigerator.

Skewer the Meat:
- Preheat your grill or braai (barbecue).
- Thread the marinated lamb cubes onto the soaked wooden skewers.

Grill Sosaties:
- Grill the sosaties over medium-high heat, turning occasionally to ensure even cooking. Brush with any remaining marinade during grilling.

Cook Until Done:
- Cook until the lamb is browned on the outside and cooked to your desired level of doneness on the inside.

Serve:

- Serve the sosaties hot as a main course or as part of a braai feast.

Sosaties are often enjoyed with sides like rice, chutney, or a fresh salad. Feel free to adapt the marinade and meat choice according to your preferences.

Potjiekos

Ingredients:

For the Potjie:

- 2-3 lbs mixed meats (beef, lamb, and/or chicken), cubed
- 2 tablespoons vegetable oil
- 2 onions, chopped
- 2 garlic cloves, minced
- 2 tablespoons curry powder
- 1 teaspoon ground coriander
- 1 teaspoon ground cumin
- 2 bay leaves
- Salt and pepper to taste
- 2 cups beef or chicken broth
- 1 cup red wine
- 4 large potatoes, peeled and sliced
- 4 carrots, peeled and sliced
- 1 cup green beans, chopped
- 2 cups butternut squash, cubed

For Garnish:

- Fresh parsley, chopped

Instructions:

Prepare the Potjie Pot:
- Heat the potjie pot over an open flame or on a braai (barbecue).

Brown the Meat:
- Heat vegetable oil in the potjie pot. Brown the cubed meat in batches, ensuring each piece gets a good sear. Remove and set aside.

Saute Onions and Garlic:
- In the same potjie pot, sauté the chopped onions and minced garlic until softened.

Add Spices:
- Stir in curry powder, ground coriander, ground cumin, bay leaves, salt, and pepper. Allow the spices to toast for a minute.

Deglaze the Pot:

- Pour in the beef or chicken broth and red wine, scraping any browned bits from the bottom of the pot to incorporate the flavors.

Layer Potatoes and Meat:
- Begin layering the sliced potatoes on the bottom of the pot. Place a layer of browned meat on top.

Add Vegetables:
- Add layers of carrots, green beans, and butternut squash.

Continue Layering:
- Continue layering until all the ingredients are used, finishing with a layer of potatoes on top.

Simmer and Cook:
- Cover the potjie pot with its lid and let it simmer over low heat for 2-3 hours or until the meat is tender and the flavors have melded. Check occasionally and add more broth if needed.

Garnish and Serve:
- Garnish with fresh chopped parsley just before serving. Serve the Potjiekos directly from the pot, allowing everyone to help themselves.

Potjiekos is a social and flavorful cooking experience, making it a popular choice for gatherings and outdoor events. Adjust the ingredients and seasoning to suit your taste preferences.

Waterblommetjie Bredie

Ingredients:

- 500g lamb or mutton, cubed
- 1 cup waterblommetjies, cleaned and trimmed
- 2 large onions, finely chopped
- 2 tablespoons vegetable oil
- 2 cloves garlic, minced
- 2 tablespoons cake flour
- 2 large carrots, peeled and sliced
- 2 large potatoes, peeled and cubed
- 2 tomatoes, chopped
- 2 tablespoons tomato paste
- 2 cups beef or lamb broth
- 1 cup red wine
- 2 bay leaves
- 1 teaspoon dried thyme
- Salt and black pepper to taste
- Fresh parsley, chopped (for garnish)

Instructions:

Prepare Waterblommetjies:
- Clean and trim the waterblommetjies, removing any tough stems or leaves.

Brown the Meat:
- In a large pot, heat vegetable oil over medium-high heat. Brown the cubed lamb or mutton in batches. Remove and set aside.

Saute Onions and Garlic:
- In the same pot, sauté the finely chopped onions and minced garlic until softened.

Add Flour:
- Sprinkle the cake flour over the onions and garlic. Stir well to create a roux.

Return Meat to Pot:
- Return the browned meat to the pot, coating it with the roux.

Add Vegetables:
- Add the sliced carrots, cubed potatoes, chopped tomatoes, and tomato paste to the pot.

Pour in Liquid:

- Pour in the beef or lamb broth and red wine. Stir to combine.

Season and Add Herbs:
- Add bay leaves, dried thyme, salt, and black pepper to taste. Stir well.

Simmer:
- Cover the pot and let the waterblommetjie bredie simmer over low heat for 1.5 to 2 hours or until the meat is tender and the flavors have melded.

Add Waterblommetjies:
- About 30 minutes before serving, add the cleaned waterblommetjies to the pot. Allow them to cook until tender but not mushy.

Adjust Seasoning:
- Taste and adjust the seasoning if necessary.

Serve:
- Garnish the waterblommetjie bredie with fresh chopped parsley just before serving. Serve it hot with rice or crusty bread.

Enjoy the unique and flavorful taste of Waterblommetjie Bredie, a dish that captures the essence of South African cuisine!

Koeksisters

Ingredients:

For the Dough:

- 4 cups all-purpose flour
- 1 tablespoon baking powder
- 1/4 teaspoon salt
- 2 tablespoons unsalted butter, softened
- 1 cup milk

For the Syrup:

- 2 cups white sugar
- 1 cup water
- 1/2 teaspoon ground cinnamon
- 1/2 teaspoon ground ginger
- Zest of 1 lemon

For Frying:

- Vegetable oil for deep frying

Instructions:

Prepare the Dough:

Mix Dry Ingredients:
- In a large bowl, sift together the all-purpose flour, baking powder, and salt.

Add Butter:
- Add the softened butter to the dry ingredients and mix until the mixture resembles coarse crumbs.

Add Milk:
- Gradually add the milk, stirring continuously until a soft dough forms.

Knead Dough:
- Turn the dough out onto a floured surface and knead it for about 5-7 minutes until smooth and elastic.

Rest Dough:
- Cover the dough with a damp cloth and let it rest for 1 hour.

Shape and Fry Koeksisters:

Roll and Cut Dough:
- Roll out the rested dough to a thickness of about 1/4 inch. Cut the dough into strips, approximately 4 inches long and 1/2 inch wide.

Braid the Strips:
- Braid three strips together to form each koeksister. Press the ends together to seal.

Heat Oil:
- Heat vegetable oil in a deep fryer or large pot to 350°F (180°C).

Deep Fry:
- Carefully lower the braided dough into the hot oil and fry until golden brown, turning occasionally to ensure even cooking. This should take about 4-5 minutes.

Drain Excess Oil:
- Remove the fried koeksisters from the oil and drain them on paper towels to absorb excess oil.

Prepare the Syrup:

Combine Ingredients:
- In a saucepan, combine sugar, water, ground cinnamon, ground ginger, and lemon zest. Bring to a boil, stirring until the sugar dissolves.

Simmer:
- Reduce the heat and let the syrup simmer for about 5-7 minutes until slightly thickened.

Soak Koeksisters:
- While the syrup is still warm, immerse each fried koeksister into the syrup, ensuring it is well coated. Allow them to soak for a few minutes.

Drain and Cool:
- Remove the koeksisters from the syrup and place them on a wire rack to drain and cool.

Enjoy these sweet and syrupy Koeksisters as a delightful treat with a cup of coffee or tea!

Durban Chicken Curry

Ingredients:

For the Curry Paste:

- 2 onions, roughly chopped
- 4 garlic cloves, minced
- 1 ginger piece (about 2 inches), peeled and chopped
- 2 tablespoons curry powder
- 1 tablespoon ground coriander
- 1 tablespoon ground cumin
- 1 teaspoon turmeric
- 1 teaspoon paprika
- 1 teaspoon chili powder (adjust to taste)
- 1 teaspoon garam masala
- 1/2 cup water (for blending)

For the Curry:

- 2-3 tablespoons vegetable oil
- 1.5 kg (3.3 lbs) chicken, cut into pieces
- 2 large tomatoes, chopped
- 1 cup plain yogurt
- 1 cup chicken broth
- Salt to taste
- Fresh coriander leaves, chopped (for garnish)

Instructions:

Prepare the Curry Paste:

Blend Ingredients:
- In a blender, combine chopped onions, minced garlic, chopped ginger, curry powder, ground coriander, ground cumin, turmeric, paprika, chili powder, garam masala, and water. Blend until you have a smooth paste.

Cook the Durban Chicken Curry:

Brown Chicken:
- Heat vegetable oil in a large pot over medium-high heat. Brown the chicken pieces in batches. Remove and set aside.

Saute Curry Paste:
- In the same pot, add more oil if needed. Add the curry paste and sauté for a few minutes until fragrant.

Add Tomatoes:
- Add the chopped tomatoes to the pot and cook until they break down and the mixture thickens.

Return Chicken to Pot:
- Return the browned chicken pieces to the pot, coating them with the curry paste.

Mix Yogurt and Broth:
- In a bowl, mix the plain yogurt with chicken broth until smooth. Pour this mixture into the pot.

Simmer:
- Bring the curry to a simmer, then reduce the heat to low. Cover and let it simmer for about 30-40 minutes until the chicken is cooked through and tender.

Adjust Seasoning:
- Taste the curry and adjust the salt if needed. You can also add more chili powder for extra heat.

Garnish and Serve:
- Garnish the Durban Chicken Curry with fresh chopped coriander leaves before serving. Serve hot with rice or bread.

Enjoy this flavorful and aromatic Durban Chicken Curry, a delicious representation of South African culinary diversity!

Chakalaka

Ingredients:

- 2 tablespoons vegetable oil
- 1 onion, finely chopped
- 1 green bell pepper, chopped
- 1 red bell pepper, chopped
- 2 carrots, grated
- 2 cloves garlic, minced
- 1 tablespoon curry powder
- 1 teaspoon ground paprika
- 1 teaspoon ground cumin
- 1 teaspoon ground coriander
- 1 can (400g) baked beans in tomato sauce
- 1 can (400g) chopped tomatoes
- 1 tablespoon tomato paste
- Salt and black pepper to taste
- Fresh parsley or cilantro, chopped (for garnish)

Instructions:

Saute Vegetables:
- Heat vegetable oil in a large skillet or pot over medium heat. Add finely chopped onions and sauté until translucent.

Add Bell Peppers and Carrots:
- Add chopped green and red bell peppers, grated carrots, and minced garlic. Cook until the vegetables are softened.

Add Spices:
- Stir in curry powder, ground paprika, ground cumin, and ground coriander. Cook for a couple of minutes to toast the spices.

Add Baked Beans and Tomatoes:
- Add baked beans in tomato sauce, chopped tomatoes, and tomato paste. Mix well to combine.

Simmer:
- Allow the mixture to simmer over low heat for about 15-20 minutes, stirring occasionally. This allows the flavors to meld and the Chakalaka to thicken.

Season:

- Season the Chakalaka with salt and black pepper to taste. Adjust the seasoning as needed.

Garnish and Serve:
- Garnish the Chakalaka with chopped fresh parsley or cilantro just before serving.

Serve:
- Serve Chakalaka as a side dish with grilled meats, roasted chicken, or as a flavorful accompaniment to bread or rice.

Chakalaka is known for its vibrant flavors and versatility. Feel free to customize the recipe by adding other vegetables or adjusting the spice levels to suit your taste preferences.

Amarula Dom Pedro

Ingredients:

- 2 shots (60ml) Amarula liqueur
- 2 scoops vanilla ice cream
- 1 shot (30ml) whiskey or brandy (optional)
- Chocolate syrup (for drizzling, optional)
- Whipped cream (for topping, optional)

Instructions:

Chill Glasses:
- Place the glasses you'll be using in the freezer to chill.

Prepare Amarula Mixture:
- In a blender, combine the Amarula liqueur, vanilla ice cream, and whiskey or brandy (if using). Blend until smooth and creamy.

Drizzle Chocolate Syrup (Optional):
- Drizzle chocolate syrup inside the chilled glasses for added flavor.

Pour Amarula Mixture:
- Pour the blended Amarula mixture into the prepared glasses.

Top with Whipped Cream (Optional):
- Top the Amarula Dom Pedro with a dollop of whipped cream if desired.

Serve:
- Serve immediately with a straw or spoon for sipping and enjoying the creamy goodness.

The Amarula Dom Pedro is a delightful after-dinner treat or a special indulgence for dessert. The combination of the smooth Amarula liqueur and creamy ice cream creates a decadent and satisfying cocktail experience.

Pap en Wors

Ingredients:

For the Pap (Maize Porridge):

- 2 cups maize meal (white or yellow)
- 4 cups water
- 1 teaspoon salt

For the Wors (Sausages):

- 6-8 boerewors sausages (a traditional South African sausage)
- Cooking oil (for frying)

Instructions:

Prepare the Pap:

    Boil Water:
- In a large pot, bring 4 cups of water to a boil.

    Add Maize Meal:
- Gradually add the maize meal to the boiling water while stirring continuously to avoid lumps.

    Stir and Simmer:
- Reduce the heat to low and continue stirring to prevent sticking. Let it simmer, covered, for about 30-40 minutes, or until the pap is cooked and has a thick, smooth consistency.

    Salt:
- Stir in salt to taste.

Cook the Wors:

    Grill or Pan-Fry:
- Grill or pan-fry the boerewors sausages until they are cooked through and have a nice browned exterior.

    Slice (Optional):
- You can either serve the sausages whole or slice them into smaller pieces.

Serve:

    Plate:

- Serve the pap and wors on individual plates.

Enjoy:
- Enjoy this simple and delicious South African meal! It's common to eat pap with your hands, using it to scoop up the sausage.

Pap en Wors is a comfort food enjoyed across South Africa, and it reflects the country's rich culinary heritage. Feel free to customize the meal by adding your favorite sauces or side dishes.

Umngqusho

Ingredients:

- 2 cups dried samp
- 1 cup sugar beans or any other dried beans of your choice
- 1 large onion, finely chopped
- 2 tablespoons vegetable oil
- 2-3 cloves garlic, minced
- 1 large tomato, chopped
- 1 teaspoon ground coriander
- 1 teaspoon ground cumin
- 1 teaspoon ground paprika
- Salt and black pepper to taste
- Fresh coriander or parsley for garnish (optional)

Instructions:

Prepare Samp and Beans:
- Rinse the dried samp and beans thoroughly under cold water. Soak them overnight or for at least 8 hours in water.

Boil Samp and Beans:
- Drain the soaked samp and beans. In a large pot, cover them with fresh water. Bring to a boil, then reduce the heat and simmer until both the samp and beans are tender. This may take 1 to 2 hours, depending on the type of samp and beans used.

Saute Onions and Garlic:
- In a separate pan, heat vegetable oil over medium heat. Add finely chopped onions and minced garlic. Sauté until the onions are translucent.

Add Spices:
- Add ground coriander, ground cumin, and ground paprika to the sautéed onions and garlic. Stir well to combine.

Add Tomatoes:
- Add the chopped tomato to the spice mixture and cook until the tomatoes are softened.

Combine Mixture:
- Combine the sautéed spice and tomato mixture with the cooked samp and beans. Mix well.

Season:

- Season with salt and black pepper to taste. Adjust the seasoning according to your preference.

Simmer:
- Allow the umngqusho to simmer over low heat for an additional 20-30 minutes, allowing the flavors to meld.

Garnish and Serve:
- Garnish with fresh coriander or parsley if desired. Serve the umngqusho hot as a side dish or as a main course.

Umngqusho is a nutritious and filling dish, often enjoyed with meat or as a standalone vegetarian meal. It holds cultural significance in South Africa and is part of the culinary heritage of the Xhosa people.

Karoo Lamb Potjie

Ingredients:

- 2 kg lamb, cut into chunks
- 2 tablespoons vegetable oil
- 2 onions, sliced
- 3 cloves garlic, minced
- 2 carrots, peeled and sliced
- 2 potatoes, peeled and cubed
- 2 tomatoes, chopped
- 2 tablespoons tomato paste
- 2 cups beef or lamb broth
- 1 cup red wine
- 2 bay leaves
- 1 teaspoon dried rosemary
- Salt and black pepper to taste
- Fresh parsley, chopped (for garnish)

Instructions:

Prepare the Potjie Pot:
- Heat the potjie pot over an open flame or on a braai (barbecue).

Brown the Lamb:
- Heat vegetable oil in the potjie pot. Brown the lamb chunks in batches. Remove and set aside.

Saute Onions and Garlic:
- In the same potjie pot, sauté the sliced onions and minced garlic until softened.

Add Vegetables:
- Add the sliced carrots, cubed potatoes, chopped tomatoes, and tomato paste to the pot. Stir well to combine.

Return Lamb to Pot:
- Return the browned lamb chunks to the pot, ensuring they are evenly distributed among the vegetables.

Pour in Liquid:
- Pour in the beef or lamb broth and red wine. Stir to combine.

Add Herbs and Seasoning:
- Add bay leaves, dried rosemary, salt, and black pepper to taste. Stir well.

Simmer:

- Cover the potjie pot with its lid and let it simmer over low heat for 2-3 hours or until the lamb is tender and the flavors have melded. Check occasionally and add more broth if needed.

Adjust Seasoning:
- Taste the stew and adjust the seasoning if necessary.

Garnish and Serve:
- Garnish the Karoo Lamb Potjie with fresh chopped parsley just before serving. Serve hot, either directly from the pot or transferred to serving plates.

Enjoy this hearty and flavorful Karoo Lamb Potjie, a dish that showcases the rich culinary traditions of South Africa. Serve it with rice, bread, or on its own as a comforting meal.

Braaibroodjies

Ingredients:

- 8 slices of bread (white or whole grain)
- Butter, softened
- 1 large tomato, thinly sliced
- 1 large onion, thinly sliced
- 1 cup grated cheddar cheese
- Salt and black pepper to taste
- Fresh basil or parsley leaves (optional, for garnish)

Instructions:

Prepare the Braai (Barbecue):
- Preheat your braai or barbecue to medium heat.

Butter the Bread:
- Spread a thin layer of softened butter on one side of each slice of bread.

Assemble the Braaibroodjies:
- On the unbuttered side of 4 slices of bread, layer tomato slices, onion slices, and grated cheddar cheese. Season with salt and black pepper to taste.

Top with Another Slice:
- Place the remaining 4 slices of bread on top, buttered side facing out.

Grill:
- Place the assembled braaibroodjies on the braai or barbecue. Grill for about 3-4 minutes on each side, or until the bread is toasted and the cheese has melted.

Check for Doneness:
- Keep an eye on the sandwiches to ensure they don't burn. The goal is to have golden-brown, crispy bread with melted cheese inside.

Serve:
- Remove the braaibroodjies from the braai and let them cool for a moment. Optionally, garnish with fresh basil or parsley leaves.

Enjoy:
- Serve the braaibroodjies warm as a tasty side dish for your braai or as a delicious snack.

Braaibroodjies are a popular addition to South African barbecues and are loved for their simplicity and savory flavors. Feel free to customize the ingredients to suit your taste, adding items like ham, bacon, or even a slice of pineapple for extra flavor variations.

Bredie

Ingredients:

- 2 lbs lamb or mutton, cut into chunks
- 2 tablespoons vegetable oil
- 2 onions, finely chopped
- 2 cloves garlic, minced
- 2 teaspoons ground coriander
- 2 teaspoons ground cumin
- 1 teaspoon ground turmeric
- 1 teaspoon paprika
- 4 large tomatoes, chopped
- 2 tablespoons tomato paste
- 3 large potatoes, peeled and diced
- 2 carrots, peeled and sliced
- Salt and black pepper to taste
- Fresh parsley, chopped (for garnish)

Instructions:

Brown the Meat:
- In a large pot or Dutch oven, heat the vegetable oil over medium heat. Brown the lamb or mutton chunks on all sides. Remove and set aside.

Saute Onions and Garlic:
- In the same pot, add more oil if needed. Saute the chopped onions and minced garlic until softened.

Add Spices:
- Stir in the ground coriander, ground cumin, ground turmeric, and paprika. Allow the spices to toast for a minute.

Return Meat to Pot:
- Return the browned meat to the pot, coating it with the onion and spice mixture.

Add Tomatoes and Tomato Paste:
- Add the chopped tomatoes and tomato paste to the pot. Stir well to combine.

Simmer:
- Allow the mixture to simmer for a few minutes, allowing the tomatoes to break down and release their juices.

Add Vegetables:

- Add the diced potatoes and sliced carrots to the pot. Mix well.

Season:
- Season the bredie with salt and black pepper to taste. Adjust the seasoning as needed.

Simmer Until Tender:
- Cover the pot and let the bredie simmer over low heat for about 1.5 to 2 hours, or until the meat is tender and the flavors have melded. Check occasionally and add water if needed.

Garnish and Serve:
- Garnish the tomato bredie with chopped fresh parsley before serving. Serve hot with rice or crusty bread.

Enjoy this comforting and hearty South African Tomato Bredie, a dish that celebrates the country's culinary heritage!

Melktert

Ingredients:

For the Pastry Crust:

- 1 1/2 cups all-purpose flour
- 1/2 cup unsalted butter, softened
- 1/3 cup sugar
- 1 large egg
- A pinch of salt

For the Filling:

- 4 cups milk
- 1 cup sugar
- 1/2 cup all-purpose flour
- 1/2 cup cornstarch
- 4 large eggs
- 1 teaspoon vanilla extract
- Cinnamon (for dusting)

Instructions:

Pastry Crust:

Preheat Oven:
- Preheat your oven to 375°F (190°C).

Prepare Pastry Dough:
- In a bowl, cream together the softened butter and sugar until light and fluffy. Add the egg and mix well. Gradually add the flour and salt, mixing until the dough comes together.

Form Crust:
- Press the pastry dough into a tart pan, covering the bottom and sides evenly. Prick the crust with a fork.

Bake:
- Bake the pastry crust in the preheated oven for about 15-20 minutes or until golden brown. Allow it to cool.

Filling:

Heat Milk:
- In a saucepan, heat the milk until it is just about to boil.

Prepare Custard Mixture:
- In a separate bowl, whisk together the sugar, flour, cornstarch, and eggs until well combined. Gradually add the hot milk to the egg mixture, stirring continuously.

Cook Custard:
- Pour the mixture back into the saucepan and cook over medium heat, stirring constantly, until the custard thickens. This may take about 5-10 minutes.

Add Vanilla:
- Remove the custard from the heat and stir in the vanilla extract.

Assemble:
- Pour the custard into the cooled pastry crust.

Chill:
- Allow the melktert to cool before placing it in the refrigerator to set for at least a few hours or overnight.

Dust with Cinnamon:
- Before serving, dust the top of the melktert with ground cinnamon.

Slice and Serve:
- Slice the melktert into wedges and serve chilled.

Enjoy this delightful South African Melktert with its creamy filling and delicate pastry crust!

Geelrys

Ingredients:

- 2 cups long-grain white rice
- 4 cups water
- 1 teaspoon turmeric
- 1 cinnamon stick
- 4 cardamom pods
- 4 whole cloves
- 1/2 teaspoon salt
- 2 tablespoons butter
- 1/2 cup raisins (optional, for added sweetness)

Instructions:

Rinse the Rice:
- Rinse the rice under cold water until the water runs clear.

Boil Water:
- In a pot, bring 4 cups of water to a boil.

Add Rice and Turmeric:
- Add the rinsed rice, turmeric, cinnamon stick, cardamom pods, whole cloves, and salt to the boiling water.

Reduce Heat and Simmer:
- Reduce the heat to low, cover the pot with a tight-fitting lid, and let the rice simmer for about 15-20 minutes, or until the rice is tender and the water has been absorbed.

Add Butter and Raisins:
- Once the rice is cooked, remove the pot from the heat. Add the butter and raisins (if using). Fluff the rice with a fork to incorporate the butter and distribute the raisins.

Rest and Serve:
- Cover the pot with a clean kitchen towel or paper towel, place the lid back on top, and let the rice rest for about 10 minutes. This allows the flavors to meld.

Fluff and Remove Spices:
- Before serving, fluff the rice again with a fork, and remove the cinnamon stick, cardamom pods, and whole cloves.

Serve:

- Serve the Geelrys as a flavorful side dish alongside your favorite meat, stew, or curry.

Geelrys adds a burst of color and flavor to your meal, making it a popular choice in South African cuisine. Adjust the sweetness by adding more or fewer raisins according to your preference.

Boeber

Ingredients:

- 1 cup vermicelli (broken into small pieces)
- 1 liter full-cream milk
- 1 cup water
- 1/2 cup sugar (adjust to taste)
- 2 cinnamon sticks
- 4 cardamom pods (crushed)
- 1 tablespoon rose water
- 1 tablespoon sago pearls (optional)
- 1 tablespoon desiccated coconut (optional)
- Ground cinnamon for garnish

Instructions:

Prepare Vermicelli:
- In a pot, add vermicelli and dry roast it until it turns golden brown. Keep an eye on it as vermicelli can quickly go from golden to burnt.

Boil Water and Add Sago (Optional):
- If you're using sago pearls, boil them separately according to the package instructions. Drain and set aside.

Boil Milk and Water:
- In a separate pot, bring the milk and water to a gentle boil.

Add Vermicelli and Spices:
- Once boiling, add the roasted vermicelli, sugar, cinnamon sticks, and crushed cardamom pods to the pot. Stir well.

Simmer:
- Reduce the heat to low and let the mixture simmer for about 15-20 minutes or until the vermicelli is cooked through and the mixture has thickened slightly.

Add Sago, Coconut, and Rose Water (Optional):
- If using sago pearls and desiccated coconut, add them to the pot at this stage. Stir in the rose water as well.

Adjust Sweetness:
- Taste and adjust the sweetness by adding more sugar if needed.

Serve:
- Remove the cinnamon sticks and cardamom pods before serving. Pour the Boeber into cups or mugs.

Garnish:
- Garnish with a sprinkle of ground cinnamon on top.

Enjoy:
- Boeber is best enjoyed warm, and it's a delightful treat, especially during cold evenings.

Boeber is not only a delicious beverage but also holds cultural significance, being associated with festive occasions and special family gatherings in South African communities.

Koeksister Ice Cream Sandwich

Ingredients:

- Koeksisters (homemade or store-bought)
- Vanilla ice cream (or any preferred flavor)
- Desiccated coconut (optional, for coating)

Instructions:

Prepare Koeksisters:
- If you're making koeksisters at home, follow your preferred recipe. Alternatively, you can purchase pre-made koeksisters from a bakery or store.

Allow Koeksisters to Cool:
- If you've just made the koeksisters, allow them to cool to room temperature. If you bought them, make sure they are at room temperature.

Prepare Ice Cream:
- Soften the vanilla ice cream slightly to make it easier to spread.

Assemble the Ice Cream Sandwiches:
- Take one koeksister and spread a generous layer of softened ice cream on one side. Place another koeksister on top, creating a sandwich. Press down gently to adhere the two pieces together.

Optional: Coat with Coconut:
- If you like, you can roll the edges of the ice cream sandwich in desiccated coconut to add an extra layer of flavor and texture.

Repeat:
- Repeat the process to make more koeksister ice cream sandwiches.

Freeze:
- Place the assembled ice cream sandwiches in the freezer for at least a couple of hours or until the ice cream is firm.

Serve and Enjoy:
- Once frozen, take the koeksister ice cream sandwiches out of the freezer, and they are ready to be enjoyed.

This South African twist on the classic ice cream sandwich is a delightful treat, combining the unique taste of koeksisters with the creamy goodness of ice cream. It's perfect for a sweet indulgence on a warm day or as a special dessert for any occasion.

Samp and Beans

Ingredients:

- 2 cups dried samp
- 1 cup dried sugar beans (or any other dried beans of your choice)
- 1 large onion, finely chopped
- 2 tablespoons vegetable oil
- 2 cloves garlic, minced
- 2 tomatoes, chopped
- 1 carrot, peeled and chopped
- 1 potato, peeled and chopped
- 1 bay leaf
- 1 teaspoon ground coriander
- 1 teaspoon ground cumin
- Salt and black pepper to taste
- Fresh parsley or coriander for garnish (optional)

Instructions:

Prepare Samp and Beans:
- Rinse the dried samp and beans separately under cold water. Soak them in water overnight or for at least 8 hours.

Boil Samp and Beans:
- Drain the soaked samp and beans. In a large pot, cover them with fresh water. Bring to a boil, then reduce the heat and simmer until both the samp and beans are tender. This may take 1 to 2 hours, depending on the type of samp and beans used.

Saute Onions and Garlic:
- In a separate pan, heat vegetable oil over medium heat. Add finely chopped onions and minced garlic. Sauté until the onions are translucent.

Add Vegetables and Spices:
- Add chopped tomatoes, carrot, potato, bay leaf, ground coriander, and ground cumin to the sautéed onions and garlic. Stir well.

Combine Mixture:
- Combine the sautéed vegetable mixture with the cooked samp and beans. Mix well.

Season:
- Season the dish with salt and black pepper to taste. Adjust the seasoning according to your preference.

Simmer:
- Let the samp and beans simmer over low heat for an additional 20-30 minutes, allowing the flavors to meld.

Garnish and Serve:
- Garnish with fresh parsley or coriander if desired. Serve hot as a side dish or as a standalone meal.

Samp and Beans is a nutritious and filling dish, deeply rooted in South African culinary traditions. It can be enjoyed on its own or as a side dish with meat or vegetables.

Tomato Bredie

Ingredients:

- 2 lbs lamb or mutton, cut into chunks
- 2 tablespoons vegetable oil
- 2 onions, finely chopped
- 2 cloves garlic, minced
- 4 large tomatoes, chopped
- 2 tablespoons tomato paste
- 2 cups beef or lamb broth
- 2 bay leaves
- 1 teaspoon dried thyme
- 1 teaspoon ground coriander
- 1 teaspoon ground cumin
- 1 teaspoon paprika
- Salt and black pepper to taste
- Fresh parsley, chopped (for garnish)

Instructions:

Brown the Meat:
- In a large pot or Dutch oven, heat the vegetable oil over medium heat. Brown the lamb or mutton chunks on all sides. Remove and set aside.

Saute Onions and Garlic:
- In the same pot, add more oil if needed. Saute the chopped onions and minced garlic until softened.

Add Tomatoes and Tomato Paste:
- Add the chopped tomatoes and tomato paste to the pot. Stir well to combine.

Return Meat to Pot:
- Return the browned meat to the pot, coating it with the tomato mixture.

Add Broth and Spices:
- Pour in the beef or lamb broth. Add bay leaves, dried thyme, ground coriander, ground cumin, paprika, salt, and black pepper to taste. Stir well.

Simmer:
- Cover the pot and let the Bredie simmer over low heat for 1.5 to 2 hours, or until the meat is tender and the flavors have melded. Check occasionally and add water if needed.

Adjust Seasoning:

- Taste the stew and adjust the seasoning if necessary.

Garnish and Serve:
- Garnish the Tomato Bredie with chopped fresh parsley before serving. Serve hot with rice or crusty bread.

Tomato Bredie is a classic South African dish that highlights the richness of tomatoes and the savory goodness of slow-cooked meat. It's a delicious and comforting option for a hearty family meal.

Vetkoek with Mince

Vetkoek Ingredients:

- 4 cups all-purpose flour
- 2 tablespoons sugar
- 1 teaspoon salt
- 1 packet (10g) instant yeast
- 1.5 cups warm water (approximately)
- Vegetable oil for deep-frying

Mince Filling Ingredients:

- 1 lb minced beef or lamb
- 1 onion, finely chopped
- 2 cloves garlic, minced
- 1 carrot, grated
- 1 tomato, chopped
- 2 tablespoons tomato paste
- 1 teaspoon ground cumin
- 1 teaspoon ground coriander
- 1 teaspoon paprika
- Salt and black pepper to taste
- Fresh parsley, chopped (for garnish)
- Vegetable oil for cooking

Instructions:

Vetkoek:

- Prepare the Dough:
    - In a large bowl, combine the flour, sugar, salt, and instant yeast. Gradually add warm water and mix until a soft dough forms. Knead the dough on a floured surface until smooth. Cover the bowl with a damp cloth and let the dough rise in a warm place until doubled in size (about 1-2 hours).
- Shape and Fry:
    - Heat vegetable oil in a deep fryer or large pot. Pinch off golf ball-sized pieces of dough, shape them into rounds, and deep-fry until golden brown. Ensure the inside is cooked by frying until the vetkoek floats and is hollow inside. Drain on paper towels.

Mince Filling:

Cook Minced Meat:
- In a separate pan, heat a bit of vegetable oil. Add chopped onions and garlic, sauté until softened. Add minced meat and cook until browned.

Add Vegetables and Spices:
- Stir in grated carrot, chopped tomato, tomato paste, ground cumin, ground coriander, paprika, salt, and black pepper. Cook until the vegetables are tender and the mixture is well combined.

Simmer:
- Simmer the mince filling for a few minutes until the flavors meld. Adjust seasoning if needed.

Assemble:
- Slice the vetkoek in half and fill each with a generous spoonful of the mince filling.

Garnish:
- Garnish with chopped fresh parsley.

Serve:
- Serve vetkoek with mince hot and enjoy!

Vetkoek with mince is a delicious and satisfying meal that captures the essence of South African comfort food.

Grilled Snoek

Ingredients:

- 1 whole snoek (cleaned and gutted)
- Olive oil
- Salt and black pepper to taste
- Lemon wedges (for serving)

Marinade Ingredients:

- 1/4 cup apricot jam
- 2 tablespoons soy sauce
- 2 tablespoons olive oil
- 2 tablespoons lemon juice
- 1 tablespoon Dijon mustard
- 2 cloves garlic, minced
- 1 teaspoon ground coriander
- 1 teaspoon ground cumin
- 1 teaspoon paprika
- 1 teaspoon dried thyme or oregano

Instructions:

Prepare the Marinade:
- In a bowl, whisk together all the marinade ingredients until well combined.

Score the Snoek:
- With a sharp knife, make diagonal cuts (scores) on both sides of the snoek. This helps the marinade to penetrate the fish, and it also allows for more even cooking.

Marinate the Snoek:
- Place the snoek in a dish or a large resealable plastic bag. Pour the marinade over the fish, ensuring it coats both sides and gets into the scores. Marinate in the refrigerator for at least 1 hour, or preferably longer for more flavor (overnight is ideal).

Preheat the Grill:
- Preheat your grill or braai to medium-high heat.

Grill the Snoek:
- Remove the snoek from the marinade and brush it with olive oil. Season with salt and black pepper. Place the snoek on the grill and cook for about

15-20 minutes, turning occasionally, until the fish is cooked through and has a nice char.

Baste with Marinade (Optional):
- If desired, you can baste the snoek with some of the leftover marinade during grilling for added flavor.

Serve:
- Once the snoek is cooked, remove it from the grill, and serve it hot. Garnish with lemon wedges.

Grilled snoek is often enjoyed with sides like rice, bread, or a fresh salad. It's a delicious way to experience the flavors of South African cuisine, especially if you love grilled fish with a touch of sweetness and savory spices.

Pickled Fish

Ingredients:

- 2 lbs firm white fish fillets (hake or snoek), cut into portions
- 1 cup all-purpose flour (for coating the fish)
- Salt and black pepper to taste
- Vegetable oil for frying

Pickling Liquid:

- 2 large onions, thinly sliced
- 2 cups white vinegar
- 1 cup water
- 1 cup sugar
- 2 tablespoons curry powder
- 1 teaspoon ground turmeric
- 1 teaspoon ground coriander
- 1 teaspoon ground cinnamon
- 1 teaspoon ground ginger
- 4-6 bay leaves
- Salt and black pepper to taste

Optional Garnish:

- Sliced lemon
- Fresh parsley, chopped

Instructions:

Prepare the Fish:
- Season the fish fillets with salt and black pepper. Coat each piece with flour.

Fry the Fish:
- Heat vegetable oil in a pan over medium heat. Fry the fish fillets until golden brown on both sides. Once cooked, set aside.

Make the Pickling Liquid:
- In a separate pot, combine the sliced onions, white vinegar, water, sugar, curry powder, ground turmeric, ground coriander, ground cinnamon, ground ginger, bay leaves, salt, and black pepper. Bring the mixture to a

> boil, then reduce the heat and let it simmer for about 10-15 minutes, allowing the flavors to meld.

Layer Fish and Pickling Liquid:
> - In a glass dish or container, layer the fried fish and the pickling liquid. Ensure the fish is well-coated. Cover the dish and refrigerate for at least 24 hours to allow the fish to absorb the flavors.

Serve:
> - Serve the pickled fish cold. Garnish with sliced lemon and chopped fresh parsley if desired.

Pickled fish is often enjoyed on its own or served with bread, rice, or as part of a spread during festive occasions. The combination of sweet, tangy, and spicy flavors makes it a unique and delightful dish in South African cuisine.

Cape Malay Chicken Curry

Ingredients:

- 2 lbs chicken pieces, skinless and bone-in
- 2 tablespoons vegetable oil
- 2 large onions, finely chopped
- 3 cloves garlic, minced
- 1 tablespoon fresh ginger, grated
- 2 tablespoons Cape Malay curry powder
- 1 teaspoon ground coriander
- 1 teaspoon ground cumin
- 1 teaspoon ground turmeric
- 1 cinnamon stick
- 2-3 cardamom pods
- 2-3 cloves
- 1 bay leaf
- 1 can (14 oz) diced tomatoes
- 1 cup chicken broth
- 2 large potatoes, peeled and cut into chunks
- Salt and black pepper to taste
- Fresh cilantro, chopped (for garnish)

Instructions:

Brown the Chicken:
- In a large pot, heat the vegetable oil over medium-high heat. Brown the chicken pieces on all sides. Remove the chicken from the pot and set it aside.

Saute Onions, Garlic, and Ginger:
- In the same pot, add more oil if needed. Saute the finely chopped onions until golden brown. Add minced garlic and grated ginger, and sauté for another 1-2 minutes.

Add Spices:
- Stir in the Cape Malay curry powder, ground coriander, ground cumin, and ground turmeric. Add the cinnamon stick, cardamom pods, cloves, and bay leaf. Cook the spices for a couple of minutes until fragrant.

Combine Tomatoes and Broth:
- Pour in the diced tomatoes and chicken broth. Stir well to combine.

Return Chicken to Pot:

- Return the browned chicken to the pot. Ensure each piece is coated with the aromatic sauce.

Simmer:
- Cover the pot and let the chicken simmer over low heat for about 30 minutes.

Add Potatoes:
- Add the potato chunks to the pot and continue simmering until both the chicken and potatoes are cooked through. Adjust the seasoning with salt and black pepper to taste.

Garnish and Serve:
- Garnish the Cape Malay Chicken Curry with chopped fresh cilantro before serving. Serve the curry over rice or with traditional Cape Malay sides like roti or sambals.

This Cape Malay Chicken Curry is rich in flavor and showcases the unique blend of spices characteristic of Cape Malay cuisine. It's a comforting and satisfying dish enjoyed by many in South Africa.

Denningvleis

Ingredients:

- 2 lbs lamb or mutton, cut into chunks
- 2 tablespoons vegetable oil
- 2 large onions, finely chopped
- 3 cloves garlic, minced
- 1/4 cup brown sugar
- 1/4 cup white vinegar
- 2 tablespoons apricot jam
- 2 tablespoons tomato paste
- 1 teaspoon ground coriander
- 1 teaspoon ground cumin
- 1 teaspoon ground cinnamon
- 1 teaspoon ground ginger
- 1 teaspoon dried chili flakes (optional for heat)
- 4-6 bay leaves
- Salt and black pepper to taste
- Fresh parsley, chopped (for garnish)
- Cooked rice or bread (for serving)

Instructions:

Brown the Meat:
- In a large pot, heat the vegetable oil over medium-high heat. Brown the lamb or mutton chunks on all sides. Remove and set aside.

Saute Onions and Garlic:
- In the same pot, add more oil if needed. Saute the chopped onions and minced garlic until softened.

Add Sweet and Sour Elements:
- Add brown sugar, white vinegar, apricot jam, and tomato paste to the pot. Stir well to combine.

Spice it Up:
- Add ground coriander, ground cumin, ground cinnamon, ground ginger, dried chili flakes (if using), bay leaves, salt, and black pepper. Mix the spices into the sweet and sour mixture.

Simmer:

- Return the browned meat to the pot. Cover the pot and let it simmer over low heat for 1.5 to 2 hours, or until the meat is tender and the flavors have melded. Check occasionally and add water if needed.

Adjust Seasoning:
- Taste the stew and adjust the seasoning if necessary. The balance of sweet and sour is key to Denningvleis.

Garnish and Serve:
- Garnish with chopped fresh parsley before serving. Serve the Denningvleis over rice or with crusty bread.

Denningvleis is a comforting and flavorful dish that reflects the diverse culinary influences in South Africa. The combination of sweet, sour, and aromatic spices makes it a unique and delicious part of Cape Malay cuisine.

Cape Malay Roti

Ingredients:

- 2 cups all-purpose flour
- 1 teaspoon salt
- 1 cup water (approximately)
- 2 tablespoons vegetable oil (plus extra for brushing)
- Butter (optional, for serving)

Instructions:

Prepare the Dough:
- In a large mixing bowl, combine the all-purpose flour and salt. Gradually add water and knead until a soft, smooth dough forms. Add more water or flour if needed to achieve the right consistency.

Add Oil:
- Drizzle the vegetable oil over the dough and continue kneading for a few more minutes until the oil is well incorporated.

Rest the Dough:
- Cover the dough with a damp cloth and let it rest for at least 30 minutes. This allows the gluten to relax, making the dough easier to roll out.

Divide and Shape:
- Divide the dough into golf ball-sized portions. Roll each portion into a smooth ball.

Roll Out the Roti:
- On a lightly floured surface, roll out each ball into a thin, flat circle. Aim for a thickness similar to that of a tortilla.

Cook the Roti:
- Heat a griddle or flat pan over medium-high heat. Place a rolled-out roti on the hot surface. Cook for about 1-2 minutes on each side, or until you see bubbles forming and the roti starting to puff up. Brush each side with a little vegetable oil during cooking.

Stack and Keep Warm:
- As each roti is cooked, stack them on a plate, and cover them with a kitchen towel to keep them warm and soft.

Serve:
- Serve Cape Malay roti warm with your favorite curry or stew. Optionally, you can spread a bit of butter on each roti before serving.

Cape Malay roti is a delightful accompaniment to curries and stews, offering a soft and slightly chewy texture. It's also great for scooping up and savoring the flavors of your favorite dishes.

Potato and Pea Curry

Ingredients:

- 3 large potatoes, peeled and diced
- 1 cup frozen or fresh peas
- 1 large onion, finely chopped
- 2 tomatoes, chopped
- 3 cloves garlic, minced
- 1-inch piece of ginger, grated
- 2 tablespoons vegetable oil
- 1 teaspoon cumin seeds
- 1 teaspoon mustard seeds
- 1 teaspoon ground turmeric
- 1 teaspoon ground cumin
- 1 teaspoon ground coriander
- 1/2 teaspoon red chili powder (adjust to taste)
- 1/2 teaspoon garam masala
- Salt to taste
- Fresh cilantro, chopped (for garnish)
- Water, as needed

Instructions:

Prepare Ingredients:
- Peel and dice the potatoes, chop the onions and tomatoes, mince the garlic, and grate the ginger.

Saute Onions and Spices:
- In a large pan, heat the vegetable oil over medium heat. Add cumin seeds and mustard seeds. When they start to splutter, add chopped onions and sauté until golden brown.

Add Garlic and Ginger:
- Add minced garlic and grated ginger to the pan. Sauté for a minute until the raw smell disappears.

Add Tomatoes:
- Add chopped tomatoes to the pan. Cook until the tomatoes are soft and the oil starts to separate from the mixture.

Add Spices:
- Stir in ground turmeric, ground cumin, ground coriander, red chili powder, and salt. Cook the spices for 1-2 minutes.

Add Potatoes and Peas:
- Add diced potatoes and peas to the pan. Mix well to coat the vegetables with the spice mixture.

Cook:
- Add enough water to cover the potatoes and peas. Cover the pan and simmer on medium-low heat until the potatoes are tender and cooked through. Stir occasionally and add more water if needed.

Finish with Garam Masala:
- Once the potatoes are cooked, sprinkle garam masala over the curry. Mix well and let it simmer for a few more minutes.

Garnish and Serve:
- Garnish the Potato and Pea Curry with chopped cilantro. Serve hot with rice or Indian bread like naan or roti.

This Potato and Pea Curry is a versatile and hearty dish that can be enjoyed as a main course or a side dish. Adjust the spice levels according to your preference.

Cape Malay Pickled Fish

Ingredients:

For the Pickling Sauce:

- 1 cup white vinegar
- 1 cup water
- 1 cup sugar
- 1 tablespoon curry powder
- 1 teaspoon ground turmeric
- 1 teaspoon ground coriander
- 1 teaspoon ground cumin
- 1 teaspoon yellow mustard seeds
- 1 teaspoon whole coriander seeds
- 1 teaspoon whole peppercorns
- 1 teaspoon salt
- 2 bay leaves

For the Fish:

- 2 lbs firm white fish fillets (such as hake or snoek), cut into portions
- All-purpose flour (for dusting)
- Vegetable oil (for frying)

Additional Ingredients:

- 2 large onions, thinly sliced
- 4 hard-boiled eggs, peeled and halved
- Fresh parsley or cilantro, chopped (for garnish)

Instructions:

Pickling Sauce:

>In a saucepan, combine all the pickling sauce ingredients.
>Bring the mixture to a boil, stirring until the sugar dissolves.
>Reduce the heat and let it simmer for about 10 minutes, allowing the flavors to meld.
>Remove the saucepan from heat and let the pickling liquid cool.

Fish:

> Dust the fish fillets with flour, shaking off any excess.
> In a pan, heat vegetable oil over medium-high heat.
> Fry the fish fillets until golden brown on both sides. Remove and drain on paper towels.

Assembly:

> In a large glass or plastic dish, layer the sliced onions.
> Place the fried fish fillets on top of the onions.
> Pour the cooled pickling liquid over the fish and onions.
> Add hard-boiled egg halves to the dish.
> Cover the dish and refrigerate for at least 24 hours, allowing the fish to absorb the flavors.

Serving:

> Garnish with fresh parsley or cilantro before serving.
> Serve the Cape Malay Pickled Fish chilled, typically with crusty bread or rice.

This dish gets better as it sits, so it's ideal to prepare it a day in advance to allow the flavors to meld. Enjoy this unique and flavorful Cape Malay Pickled Fish!

Ostrich Bobotie

Ingredients:

For the Bobotie:

- 1 lb ground ostrich meat
- 2 slices white bread, crusts removed
- 1 cup milk
- 1 large onion, finely chopped
- 2 cloves garlic, minced
- 2 tablespoons vegetable oil
- 2 tablespoons curry powder
- 1 tablespoon apricot jam
- 1 tablespoon chutney
- 1 tablespoon white vinegar
- 1 teaspoon turmeric
- 1 teaspoon ground coriander
- 1 teaspoon ground cumin
- Salt and black pepper to taste
- 1/4 cup raisins or sultanas
- 1/4 cup almonds, slivered
- Butter for greasing the baking dish

For the Topping:

- 2 large eggs
- 1 cup milk
- Pinch of salt

For Garnish:

- Fresh bay leaves (optional)

Instructions:

Preheat Oven:
- Preheat your oven to 350°F (180°C).

Prepare Bread Soak:
- In a bowl, soak the bread slices in 1 cup of milk until softened.

Prepare Bobotie Mixture:

- In a pan, heat vegetable oil over medium heat. Add chopped onions and garlic, sauté until softened.
- Add curry powder, apricot jam, chutney, white vinegar, turmeric, ground coriander, and ground cumin. Mix well.
- Add the ground ostrich meat and cook until browned.
- Squeeze excess milk from the soaked bread and add the bread to the meat mixture. Stir well to combine.
- Season with salt and black pepper. Add raisins or sultanas and slivered almonds. Mix thoroughly.

Transfer to Baking Dish:
- Grease a baking dish with butter. Transfer the ostrich bobotie mixture to the dish, spreading it evenly.

Prepare Topping:
- In a bowl, whisk together eggs, milk, and a pinch of salt. Pour the egg mixture over the meat mixture.

Bake:
- Bake in the preheated oven for about 30-40 minutes or until the topping is set and golden brown.

Garnish:
- If desired, garnish with fresh bay leaves for decoration.

Serve:
- Serve the ostrich bobotie hot, typically with yellow rice and chutney.

Ostrich bobotie offers a lean and flavorful alternative to the traditional beef or lamb bobotie, and it showcases the unique flavors of South African cuisine.

Cape Malay Samoosas

Ingredients:

For the Filling:

- 1 lb minced lamb or beef
- 1 large onion, finely chopped
- 2 tablespoons vegetable oil
- 2 teaspoons Cape Malay curry powder
- 1 teaspoon ground cumin
- 1 teaspoon ground coriander
- 1 teaspoon ground turmeric
- 1 teaspoon ginger, minced
- 1 teaspoon garlic, minced
- 1 cup frozen peas
- Salt and black pepper to taste
- Fresh cilantro, chopped (optional)

For the Pastry:

- 2 cups all-purpose flour
- 1/4 cup vegetable oil
- Water (for dough)
- Oil (for frying)

Instructions:

For the Filling:

Prepare the Meat:
- In a pan, heat vegetable oil over medium heat. Add chopped onions and sauté until softened.
- Add minced meat and cook until browned.

Add Spices:
- Add Cape Malay curry powder, ground cumin, ground coriander, ground turmeric, minced ginger, and minced garlic. Stir well.

Add Peas:
- Add frozen peas and cook for a few more minutes until they are heated through.

Season:
- Season with salt and black pepper. Adjust the seasoning to taste.

Finish with Cilantro:

- If using, stir in chopped fresh cilantro for added flavor. Remove the filling from heat and let it cool.

For the Pastry:

Prepare the Dough:
- In a mixing bowl, combine all-purpose flour and vegetable oil. Gradually add water and knead until you form a soft, pliable dough. Let it rest for about 30 minutes.

Form the Samoosas:
- Divide the dough into small balls. Roll each ball into a thin, round disc.

Fill and Seal:
- Place a spoonful of the cooled filling on one half of the disc. Fold the other half over the filling to form a triangle. Press the edges to seal.

Fry:
- Heat oil in a deep pan or fryer. Fry the samoosas until they are golden brown and crispy. Ensure the oil is hot enough to cook the samoosas quickly.

Drain and Serve:
- Remove the samoosas from the oil and drain on paper towels.

Serve:
- Serve Cape Malay samoosas hot, either on their own or with a dipping sauce like chutney or yogurt.

These Cape Malay samoosas are not only delicious but also carry the unique flavors of Cape Malay cuisine. They make for excellent appetizers or snacks during gatherings.

Amasi Chicken

Ingredients:

- 1 whole chicken, cut into pieces
- 2 cups amasi (fermented milk)
- 2 tablespoons vegetable oil
- 1 large onion, finely chopped
- 2 tomatoes, chopped
- 2 tablespoons tomato paste
- 2 teaspoons ground coriander
- 2 teaspoons ground cumin
- 1 teaspoon ground turmeric
- 1 teaspoon paprika
- 1 teaspoon ground ginger
- 3 cloves garlic, minced
- Salt and black pepper to taste
- Fresh cilantro or parsley, chopped (for garnish)
- Cooked rice or bread (for serving)

Instructions:

Marinate the Chicken:
- In a large bowl, mix the chicken pieces with half of the amasi. Allow the chicken to marinate for at least 30 minutes, or preferably, overnight in the refrigerator.

Cook the Chicken:
- Heat vegetable oil in a large pot or skillet over medium heat. Add the chopped onions and sauté until softened.

Add Spices:
- Stir in the ground coriander, ground cumin, ground turmeric, paprika, ground ginger, and minced garlic. Cook for a couple of minutes until the spices release their aroma.

Cook Chicken:
- Add the marinated chicken pieces to the pot, along with the remaining amasi. Cook until the chicken is browned on all sides.

Add Tomatoes and Tomato Paste:
- Add the chopped tomatoes and tomato paste to the pot. Stir well to combine.

Simmer:

- Reduce the heat to low, cover the pot, and let the chicken simmer in the amasi and tomato mixture until it's cooked through. This may take around 30-40 minutes.

Season:
- Season with salt and black pepper to taste. Adjust the seasoning if needed.

Garnish and Serve:
- Garnish the Amasi Chicken with chopped fresh cilantro or parsley. Serve the dish hot with rice or bread.

Amasi Chicken is known for its rich and tangy flavor, and it's a delightful way to experience the use of fermented milk in South African cuisine. Enjoy this unique and comforting dish!

South African Milk Tart

Ingredients:

For the Crust:

- 1 1/2 cups all-purpose flour
- 1/2 cup unsalted butter, softened
- 1/2 cup sugar
- 1 large egg
- 1 teaspoon baking powder
- A pinch of salt

For the Filling:

- 4 cups milk
- 1 cup sugar
- 1/2 cup all-purpose flour
- 1/2 cup cornstarch
- 4 large eggs
- 1 teaspoon vanilla extract
- A pinch of salt
- Ground cinnamon (for dusting)

Instructions:

For the Crust:

Preheat Oven:
- Preheat your oven to 350°F (180°C).

Prepare Crust:
- In a bowl, cream together softened butter and sugar until light and fluffy. Add the egg and beat until well combined.

Add Dry Ingredients:
- Sift in the flour, baking powder, and a pinch of salt. Mix until a soft dough forms.

Press into Pan:
- Press the dough into a tart or pie pan, covering the bottom and sides evenly. Use your fingers to create a smooth, even crust.

Bake:

- Bake the crust in the preheated oven for about 15 minutes or until it is lightly golden. Remove from the oven and let it cool while you prepare the filling.

For the Filling:

Mix Dry Ingredients:
- In a bowl, whisk together sugar, flour, cornstarch, and a pinch of salt.

Whisk in Eggs:
- In a separate bowl, whisk together the eggs. Add the eggs to the dry ingredients and whisk until well combined.

Heat Milk:
- In a saucepan, heat the milk until it is just about to boil.

Combine and Cook:
- Slowly pour the hot milk into the egg mixture, whisking continuously to avoid scrambling the eggs. Once combined, pour the mixture back into the saucepan.

Cook Until Thickened:
- Cook the mixture over medium heat, stirring constantly, until it thickens. This should take about 10-15 minutes.

Add Vanilla:
- Remove the mixture from heat and stir in the vanilla extract. Let it cool for a few minutes.

Assemble and Chill:
- Pour the custard into the pre-baked crust. Smooth the top with a spatula. Allow it to cool to room temperature, then refrigerate for at least 2-3 hours or until set.

Dust with Cinnamon:
- Before serving, dust the top of the Milk Tart with ground cinnamon.

South African Milk Tart is best served chilled, and its creamy texture and sweet, cinnamon-kissed flavor make it a beloved dessert in South Africa.

Tomato Smoor

Ingredients:

- 2 tablespoons vegetable oil
- 1 large onion, finely chopped
- 2 cloves garlic, minced
- 1 teaspoon ground cumin
- 1 teaspoon ground coriander
- 1 teaspoon paprika
- 1/2 teaspoon ground turmeric
- 1/2 teaspoon ground cinnamon
- 1/4 teaspoon cayenne pepper (optional, for heat)
- 1 kg ripe tomatoes, chopped (about 4-5 large tomatoes)
- 1 tablespoon tomato paste
- 1 teaspoon sugar
- Salt and black pepper to taste
- Fresh cilantro or parsley, chopped (for garnish)

Instructions:

Saute Onions and Garlic:
- Heat vegetable oil in a large skillet or pot over medium heat. Add chopped onions and sauté until softened.

Add Spices:
- Stir in minced garlic, ground cumin, ground coriander, paprika, ground turmeric, ground cinnamon, and cayenne pepper (if using). Cook for a couple of minutes until the spices release their aroma.

Add Tomatoes:
- Add the chopped tomatoes to the pot. Stir well to combine.

Cook Down Tomatoes:
- Allow the tomatoes to cook down for about 10-15 minutes, stirring occasionally. The tomatoes should soften and release their juices.

Add Tomato Paste and Sugar:
- Stir in the tomato paste and sugar. Mix well to incorporate.

Simmer:
- Reduce the heat to low, cover the pot, and let the mixture simmer for an additional 15-20 minutes, or until the tomatoes are fully cooked and the flavors have melded.

Season:

- Season the Tomato Smoor with salt and black pepper to taste. Adjust the seasoning if needed.

Garnish and Serve:
- Garnish the Tomato Smoor with chopped fresh cilantro or parsley before serving.

Serve:
- Tomato Smoor can be served as a side dish alongside rice, bread, or as a topping for grilled meats. It's delicious both warm and at room temperature.

Tomato Smoor is a versatile and flavorful dish that highlights the natural sweetness of ripe tomatoes combined with aromatic spices. Enjoy this South African delight as part of your meal!

Cape Malay Snoek Pâté

Ingredients:

- 250g smoked snoek, deboned and flaked
- 1 small onion, finely chopped
- 2 tablespoons butter
- 1 teaspoon ground coriander
- 1 teaspoon ground cumin
- 1 teaspoon mild curry powder
- 1/2 teaspoon turmeric
- 1/4 teaspoon ground cinnamon
- 1/4 teaspoon ground cloves
- 1/4 teaspoon ground allspice
- 1 tablespoon lemon juice
- 1/2 cup mayonnaise
- 1/4 cup plain yogurt
- Salt and pepper to taste
- Fresh coriander or parsley, chopped (for garnish)
- Lemon wedges (for serving)
- Crackers or bread (for serving)

Instructions:

Prepare Smoked Snoek:
- Ensure the smoked snoek is deboned and flaked. Remove any skin or bones as needed.

Saute Onions:
- In a pan, sauté the finely chopped onion in butter until soft and translucent.

Add Spices:
- Add ground coriander, ground cumin, curry powder, turmeric, ground cinnamon, ground cloves, and ground allspice to the sautéed onions. Cook for a couple of minutes until the spices release their aroma.

Combine with Snoek:
- Add the flaked smoked snoek to the pan. Mix well with the spiced onions.

Add Lemon Juice:
- Stir in lemon juice to add a bright, citrusy flavor to the mixture.

Make Pâté Base:

- Transfer the snoek and spice mixture to a food processor. Add mayonnaise and plain yogurt. Process until you achieve a smooth pâté consistency.

Season:
- Season the pâté with salt and pepper to taste. Adjust the seasoning if necessary.

Chill:
- Transfer the pâté to a bowl, cover, and refrigerate for at least 1-2 hours to allow the flavors to meld.

Garnish and Serve:
- Before serving, garnish the Cape Malay Snoek Pâté with chopped fresh coriander or parsley.

Serve:
- Serve the pâté chilled with lemon wedges and your choice of crackers or bread.

Cape Malay Snoek Pâté is a delicious appetizer or snack that showcases the rich flavors of Cape Malay cuisine. It's perfect for gatherings or as a tasty treat for yourself.

Cape Malay Tomato Bredie

Ingredients:

- 1.5 kg lamb stew meat, cut into chunks
- 2 tablespoons vegetable oil
- 2 large onions, finely chopped
- 3 cloves garlic, minced
- 2 teaspoons ground coriander
- 2 teaspoons ground cumin
- 1 teaspoon ground cinnamon
- 1 teaspoon ground ginger
- 1 teaspoon ground turmeric
- 1 teaspoon paprika
- 1/2 teaspoon cayenne pepper (optional, for heat)
- 4 large tomatoes, chopped
- 2 tablespoons tomato paste
- 2 cups beef or lamb broth
- 1 cinnamon stick
- 4-6 cardamom pods
- Salt and black pepper to taste
- Fresh cilantro, chopped (for garnish)
- Cooked rice or bread (for serving)

Instructions:

Brown the Lamb:
- In a large pot, heat vegetable oil over medium-high heat. Brown the lamb stew meat on all sides. Remove and set aside.

Saute Onions and Spices:
- In the same pot, add more oil if needed. Saute the chopped onions until softened. Add minced garlic and sauté for another minute.
- Add ground coriander, ground cumin, ground cinnamon, ground ginger, ground turmeric, paprika, and cayenne pepper (if using). Stir well to coat the onions in the spices.

Add Tomatoes and Tomato Paste:
- Add the chopped tomatoes and tomato paste to the pot. Stir and cook for a few minutes until the tomatoes start to break down.

Combine Lamb and Broth:

- Return the browned lamb to the pot. Pour in the beef or lamb broth. Stir well to combine.

Add Aromatics:
- Add a cinnamon stick and cardamom pods to the pot. These aromatics will infuse the stew with flavor.

Simmer:
- Reduce the heat to low, cover the pot, and let the Tomato Bredie simmer for about 1.5 to 2 hours, or until the lamb is tender and the flavors have melded.

Season:
- Season the stew with salt and black pepper to taste. Adjust the seasoning if needed.

Garnish and Serve:
- Garnish the Cape Malay Tomato Bredie with chopped fresh cilantro. Serve the stew hot with cooked rice or bread.

Cape Malay Tomato Bredie is a comforting and flavorful stew that reflects the rich culinary heritage of Cape Malay cuisine. Enjoy it as a hearty meal on its own or with your favorite accompaniments.

Amarula Malva Pudding

Ingredients:

For the Pudding:

- 1 cup all-purpose flour
- 1 cup sugar
- 1 teaspoon baking soda
- 1/4 teaspoon salt
- 1 large egg
- 1 tablespoon apricot jam
- 1 tablespoon melted butter
- 1 teaspoon vinegar
- 1 cup milk

For the Sauce:

- 1 cup heavy cream
- 1/2 cup butter
- 1/2 cup sugar
- 1/2 cup Amarula liqueur

Instructions:

For the Pudding:

Preheat Oven:
- Preheat your oven to 350°F (180°C). Grease a baking dish.

Mix Dry Ingredients:
- In a bowl, whisk together the flour, sugar, baking soda, and salt.

Add Wet Ingredients:
- In another bowl, beat the egg and then add the apricot jam, melted butter, vinegar, and milk. Mix well.

Combine Wet and Dry:
- Gradually add the wet ingredients to the dry ingredients, stirring until well combined.

Bake:
- Pour the batter into the greased baking dish and bake in the preheated oven for about 30-35 minutes or until the pudding is golden brown and set.

For the Sauce:

- Prepare Sauce:
  - While the pudding is baking, prepare the sauce. In a saucepan, combine the heavy cream, butter, sugar, and Amarula liqueur.
- Heat and Simmer:
  - Heat the sauce over medium heat, stirring until the butter and sugar are melted. Allow the sauce to simmer for a few minutes until it thickens slightly.
- Pour Sauce Over Pudding:
  - Once the pudding is out of the oven, immediately pour the warm sauce over the hot pudding, allowing it to soak in.
- Serve:
  - Allow the Amarula Malva Pudding to rest for a few minutes before serving. Serve the pudding warm, and optionally, you can serve it with a scoop of vanilla ice cream or a dollop of whipped cream.

Enjoy the rich and indulgent flavors of Amarula Malva Pudding, a delightful South African treat!

Cape Malay Lamb Biryani

Ingredients:

For the Lamb Marinade:

- 1.5 kg lamb, cut into chunks
- 1 cup plain yogurt
- 2 tablespoons ginger-garlic paste
- 1 tablespoon ground coriander
- 1 tablespoon ground cumin
- 1 tablespoon ground turmeric
- 1 tablespoon garam masala
- 1 tablespoon paprika
- Salt to taste
- Fresh coriander and mint leaves, chopped (for garnish)

For the Rice:

- 3 cups basmati rice, soaked for 30 minutes and drained
- Water for cooking rice
- 2 bay leaves
- 4-5 whole cloves
- 4-5 whole green cardamom pods
- 2-inch cinnamon stick
- Salt to taste

For the Biryani:

- 3 large onions, thinly sliced
- 1/2 cup vegetable oil or ghee
- 2 tomatoes, chopped
- 1/2 cup fried onions (for garnish)
- Fresh coriander and mint leaves, chopped (for garnish)

Instructions:

Lamb Marinade:

    Marinate the Lamb:

- In a large bowl, mix together the yogurt, ginger-garlic paste, ground coriander, ground cumin, ground turmeric, garam masala, paprika, and salt.
- Add the lamb chunks to the marinade, ensuring they are well-coated. Cover and refrigerate for at least 2 hours or overnight for maximum flavor.

Rice:

Cook the Rice:
- In a large pot, bring water to boil. Add soaked and drained basmati rice, bay leaves, whole cloves, green cardamom pods, cinnamon stick, and salt.
- Cook the rice until it's about 70% cooked (it should still have a slight bite). Drain the rice and set aside.

Biryani:

Fry Onions:
- In a large, heavy-bottomed pot, heat vegetable oil or ghee. Fry the thinly sliced onions until golden brown and crispy. Remove some fried onions for garnish.

Cook Marinated Lamb:
- Add the marinated lamb to the pot with the remaining fried onions. Cook until the lamb is browned and cooked through.

Layering:
- Layer the partially cooked rice over the cooked lamb in the pot. Sprinkle chopped tomatoes on top.

Finish Layering:
- Add a layer of fried onions, and sprinkle with fresh coriander and mint leaves.

Dum Cooking (Steam Cooking):
- Cover the pot with a tight-fitting lid. Place a damp cloth or aluminum foil over the pot before putting on the lid to trap steam.
- Cook on low heat for about 30-40 minutes or until the rice is fully cooked and the flavors have melded.

Serve:
- Gently fluff the biryani with a fork. Serve Cape Malay Lamb Biryani hot, garnished with fried onions, fresh coriander, and mint leaves.

Cape Malay Lamb Biryani is a fragrant and flavorful dish that brings together the rich culinary traditions of the Cape Malay community. Enjoy this aromatic biryani with your favorite raita or yogurt sauce.

Samp and Lamb Stew

Ingredients:

For the Lamb Marinade:

- 1.5 kg lamb stew meat, cut into chunks
- 2 tablespoons vegetable oil
- 1 large onion, finely chopped
- 2 teaspoons ground coriander
- 2 teaspoons ground cumin
- 1 teaspoon ground paprika
- 1 teaspoon ground turmeric
- Salt and black pepper to taste

For the Stew:

- 2 cups samp, soaked overnight and drained
- Water for cooking samp
- 2 tablespoons vegetable oil
- 2 large onions, finely chopped
- 3 cloves garlic, minced
- 2 teaspoons ground coriander
- 2 teaspoons ground cumin
- 1 teaspoon ground paprika
- 1 teaspoon ground turmeric
- 2 large carrots, peeled and diced
- 2 large potatoes, peeled and diced
- 4 tomatoes, chopped
- 1 cinnamon stick
- 4-6 whole cloves
- 4-6 whole cardamom pods
- 1 bay leaf
- 4 cups beef or lamb broth
- Salt and black pepper to taste
- Fresh parsley, chopped (for garnish)

Instructions:

Lamb Marinade:

Marinate the Lamb:
- In a bowl, combine lamb stew meat with vegetable oil, chopped onions, ground coriander, ground cumin, ground paprika, ground turmeric, salt, and black pepper. Allow the lamb to marinate for at least 30 minutes.

Samp:

Cook the Samp:
- In a large pot, bring water to boil. Add soaked and drained samp. Cook until the samp is tender but still has a slight bite. Drain and set aside.

Stew:

Saute Onions and Spices:
- In a large, heavy-bottomed pot, heat vegetable oil. Saute chopped onions until softened. Add minced garlic, ground coriander, ground cumin, ground paprika, and ground turmeric. Cook for a couple of minutes until the spices release their aroma.

Brown the Marinated Lamb:
- Add the marinated lamb to the pot. Brown the meat on all sides.

Add Vegetables:
- Stir in diced carrots, diced potatoes, and chopped tomatoes.

Spices and Aromatics:
- Add the cinnamon stick, whole cloves, whole cardamom pods, bay leaf, and beef or lamb broth to the pot. Season with salt and black pepper to taste.

Simmer:
- Bring the stew to a boil, then reduce the heat to low. Cover the pot and let it simmer for about 1.5 to 2 hours or until the lamb is tender and the flavors have melded.

Add Cooked Samp:
- Once the lamb is tender, add the cooked samp to the stew. Stir gently to combine.

Final Seasoning:
- Taste and adjust the seasoning if needed. Remove the cinnamon stick, cloves, cardamom pods, and bay leaf.

Serve:
- Serve Samp and Lamb Stew hot, garnished with chopped fresh parsley.

Samp and Lamb Stew is a wholesome and comforting dish that combines the earthy taste of samp with the rich flavors of lamb and aromatic spices. Enjoy it as a hearty meal on its own.

Rooibos-Infused Salmon

Ingredients:

- 4 salmon fillets
- 2 cups strongly brewed rooibos tea, cooled
- 2 tablespoons honey
- 2 tablespoons soy sauce
- 2 cloves garlic, minced
- 1 teaspoon grated ginger
- 1 tablespoon olive oil
- Salt and black pepper to taste
- Fresh lemon wedges (for serving)
- Fresh parsley or cilantro, chopped (for garnish)

Instructions:

Prepare Rooibos Infusion:
- Brew a strong cup of rooibos tea and allow it to cool completely.

Prepare Marinade:
- In a bowl, whisk together the cooled rooibos tea, honey, soy sauce, minced garlic, grated ginger, olive oil, salt, and black pepper. This will be your marinade.

Marinate the Salmon:
- Place the salmon fillets in a shallow dish or a resealable plastic bag. Pour the rooibos marinade over the salmon, making sure it's well-coated. Seal the bag or cover the dish and refrigerate for at least 30 minutes, allowing the flavors to infuse.

Preheat Oven or Grill:
- Preheat your oven to 375°F (190°C) or prepare a grill.

Cook the Salmon:
- If using an oven, place the marinated salmon on a baking sheet lined with parchment paper. Bake for about 15-20 minutes or until the salmon is cooked to your liking.
- If using a grill, preheat it to medium-high heat. Grill the salmon for about 4-6 minutes per side, depending on thickness, until the salmon is cooked through and has grill marks.

Baste with Marinade:
- While cooking, you can baste the salmon with the reserved marinade to enhance the flavor.

Serve:
- Once cooked, transfer the salmon to a serving platter. Garnish with chopped fresh parsley or cilantro and serve with lemon wedges on the side.

Enjoy:
- Rooibos-Infused Salmon is best enjoyed hot, and it pairs well with a side of steamed vegetables, rice, or quinoa.

This dish offers a delightful combination of the smoky and herbal notes from rooibos tea, complementing the natural richness of salmon. It's a unique and flavorful way to enjoy this popular fish.

Peppermint Crisp Tart

Ingredients:

For the Base:

- 250g (about 2 cups) digestive biscuits or tennis biscuits, crushed
- 125g (1/2 cup) unsalted butter, melted

For the Caramel Layer:

- 1 can (397g) sweetened condensed milk
- 2 tablespoons unsalted butter
- Pinch of salt

For the Peppermint Crisp Layer:

- 4 Peppermint Crisp chocolate bars (about 150g each), crushed

For the Whipped Cream Layer:

- 2 cups heavy whipping cream
- 2 tablespoons powdered sugar
- 1 teaspoon vanilla extract

Instructions:

Base:

Crush Biscuits:
- Crush the digestive biscuits or tennis biscuits into fine crumbs. You can use a food processor or place the biscuits in a zip-top bag and crush them with a rolling pin.

Mix with Melted Butter:
- Combine the crushed biscuits with melted unsalted butter, making sure the crumbs are well-coated.

Press into Pan:
- Press the biscuit mixture into the base of a tart or pie dish to form an even crust. Use the back of a spoon to compact the base. Place the dish in the refrigerator to set while you prepare the other layers.

Caramel Layer:

Prepare Caramel:
- In a saucepan, melt the unsalted butter. Add the sweetened condensed milk and a pinch of salt. Cook over medium heat, stirring continuously, until the mixture thickens and turns a golden caramel color. Be careful not to burn it.

Pour over Biscuit Base:
- Pour the caramel over the chilled biscuit base and spread it evenly. Allow it to cool and set in the refrigerator.

Peppermint Crisp Layer:

Crush Peppermint Crisp Bars:
- Crush the Peppermint Crisp chocolate bars into small pieces.

Sprinkle over Caramel:
- Sprinkle the crushed Peppermint Crisp over the caramel layer.

Whipped Cream Layer:

Whip Cream:
- In a separate bowl, whip the heavy whipping cream until stiff peaks form. Add powdered sugar and vanilla extract, and continue to whip until well combined.

Spread over Peppermint Crisp Layer:
- Spread the whipped cream over the Peppermint Crisp layer, covering the tart evenly.

Chill:
- Refrigerate the Peppermint Crisp Tart for at least 4 hours or overnight to allow all the layers to set.

Serve:
- Once chilled and set, slice the Peppermint Crisp Tart into portions and serve.

This indulgent Peppermint Crisp Tart is a favorite at South African gatherings, offering a delightful combination of textures and flavors. Enjoy the layers of sweetness and crunch!

Biltong and Cheese Quiche

Ingredients:

For the Quiche Filling:

- 1 cup biltong, finely chopped
- 1 cup grated cheddar cheese
- 1/2 cup grated Parmesan cheese
- 1 small onion, finely chopped
- 1 tablespoon olive oil
- 4 large eggs
- 1 cup milk
- Salt and black pepper to taste
- 1 tablespoon fresh parsley, chopped (optional)

For the Quiche Crust:

- 1 1/2 cups all-purpose flour
- 1/2 cup cold unsalted butter, diced
- 1/4 cup grated Parmesan cheese
- 2-3 tablespoons ice water

Instructions:

Quiche Crust:

   Prepare Crust Dough:
   - In a food processor, combine the all-purpose flour, cold diced butter, and grated Parmesan cheese. Pulse until the mixture resembles coarse crumbs.

   Add Ice Water:
   - Gradually add ice water, one tablespoon at a time, while pulsing, until the dough just comes together.

   Form Dough:
   - Turn the dough out onto a lightly floured surface and knead it briefly to bring it together. Shape it into a disk, wrap it in plastic wrap, and refrigerate for at least 30 minutes.

   Roll Out Crust:
   - Preheat the oven to 375°F (190°C). Roll out the chilled dough on a floured surface and fit it into a greased quiche or tart pan. Trim any excess dough hanging over the edges.

   Blind Bake:

- Line the crust with parchment paper and fill it with pie weights or dried beans. Blind bake the crust for about 15 minutes in the preheated oven. Remove the parchment paper and weights and bake for an additional 5 minutes, or until lightly golden. Set aside.

Quiche Filling:

Saute Onions:
- In a skillet, heat olive oil over medium heat. Saute the finely chopped onion until softened.

Prepare Filling Mixture:
- In a bowl, whisk together the eggs and milk. Add the sauteed onions, chopped biltong, grated cheddar cheese, grated Parmesan cheese, salt, black pepper, and chopped fresh parsley. Mix well.

Assemble Quiche:
- Pour the filling mixture into the pre-baked quiche crust.

Bake:
- Bake the quiche in the preheated oven for 25-30 minutes or until the filling is set and the top is golden brown.

Cool and Serve:
- Allow the Biltong and Cheese Quiche to cool slightly before slicing. Serve warm or at room temperature.

Enjoy the unique and savory flavors of Biltong and Cheese Quiche as a delightful addition to your brunch or lunch menu!

Koeksister Bread Pudding

Ingredients:

For the Koeksister Syrup:

- 1 cup sugar
- 1/2 cup water
- 1/2 teaspoon lemon juice
- 1/2 teaspoon ground cinnamon
- 1/2 teaspoon ground ginger

For the Bread Pudding:

- 6-8 stale koeksisters, cut into bite-sized pieces
- 6 cups stale bread, cubed
- 4 large eggs
- 2 cups whole milk
- 1 cup heavy cream
- 1 cup sugar
- 1 teaspoon vanilla extract
- Pinch of salt
- Butter (for greasing the baking dish)

Instructions:

Koeksister Syrup:

Prepare Syrup:
- In a saucepan, combine sugar, water, lemon juice, ground cinnamon, and ground ginger. Bring the mixture to a simmer over medium heat, stirring until the sugar dissolves.

Simmer:
- Allow the syrup to simmer for 5-7 minutes, or until it slightly thickens. Remove from heat and let it cool. The syrup will thicken further as it cools.

Bread Pudding:

Preheat Oven:
- Preheat your oven to 350°F (175°C). Grease a baking dish with butter.

Prepare Koeksisters and Bread:

- Cut stale koeksisters into bite-sized pieces and cube the stale bread.

Layer the Baking Dish:
- Place a layer of cubed koeksisters in the greased baking dish, followed by a layer of cubed bread. Repeat until all the koeksisters and bread are used, creating a layered effect.

Make Custard Mixture:
- In a bowl, whisk together eggs, whole milk, heavy cream, sugar, vanilla extract, and a pinch of salt until well combined.

Pour Custard Over Layers:
- Pour the custard mixture over the layered koeksisters and bread, ensuring that the liquid covers the top layer.

Soak:
- Allow the bread pudding to soak for about 15-20 minutes, allowing the custard to be absorbed by the bread and koeksisters.

Bake:
- Bake in the preheated oven for 40-45 minutes, or until the top is golden brown and the custard is set.

Drizzle with Koeksister Syrup:
- Once out of the oven, drizzle the prepared koeksister syrup over the hot bread pudding, ensuring it soaks into the layers.

Serve:
- Allow the Koeksister Bread Pudding to cool slightly before serving. Serve warm, optionally with a scoop of vanilla ice cream or a dollop of whipped cream.

This Koeksister Bread Pudding combines the sweetness of koeksisters with the comforting texture of bread pudding for a delicious and indulgent treat. Enjoy the South African flavors!

Peri-Peri Chicken

Ingredients:

For the Peri-Peri Sauce:

- 1/4 cup olive oil
- 4-6 cloves garlic, minced
- 2-3 red chili peppers, finely chopped (adjust according to spice preference)
- 1 teaspoon smoked paprika
- 1 teaspoon dried oregano
- 1 teaspoon ground cumin
- 1/2 cup red wine vinegar
- Juice of 1 lemon
- Salt and black pepper to taste

For the Chicken:

- 4-6 chicken leg quarters or a whole chicken, cut into pieces
- Salt and black pepper to taste
- Olive oil for basting

Instructions:

Peri-Peri Sauce:

   Prepare the Sauce:
   - In a saucepan, heat olive oil over medium heat. Add minced garlic and chopped red chili peppers. Saute for a few minutes until the garlic is fragrant.

   Add Spices:
   - Stir in smoked paprika, dried oregano, and ground cumin. Cook for an additional minute to release the flavors.

   Deglaze with Vinegar and Lemon Juice:
   - Pour in red wine vinegar and lemon juice to deglaze the pan, scraping any flavorful bits from the bottom. Simmer for a few minutes until the sauce thickens slightly.

   Season:
   - Season the peri-peri sauce with salt and black pepper to taste. Remove from heat and let it cool.

Chicken:

- Marinate Chicken:
    - Season the chicken pieces with salt and black pepper. Place the chicken in a large bowl or zip-top bag.
- Coat with Peri-Peri Sauce:
    - Pour the cooled peri-peri sauce over the chicken, ensuring that all pieces are well-coated. Marinate in the refrigerator for at least 2 hours or overnight for maximum flavor.
- Preheat Grill or Oven:
    - Preheat your grill or oven to medium-high heat.
- Grill or Roast:
    - If using a grill, place the chicken on the preheated grill and cook for about 30-40 minutes, turning occasionally and basting with olive oil. Cook until the chicken reaches an internal temperature of 165°F (74°C).
    - If using an oven, preheat to 400°F (200°C). Place the marinated chicken in a roasting pan and roast for about 45-60 minutes, basting with olive oil, until the chicken is cooked through.
- Serve:
    - Once cooked, transfer the Peri-Peri Chicken to a serving platter. Garnish with fresh herbs and serve hot.

Peri-Peri Chicken is known for its bold and spicy flavors, making it a favorite for those who enjoy a bit of heat. Serve it with sides like rice, coleslaw, or grilled vegetables for a complete and satisfying meal.

Vetkoek with Avo and Biltong

Ingredients:

For the Vetkoek:

- 3 cups all-purpose flour
- 1 tablespoon sugar
- 1 teaspoon salt
- 1 packet (10g) instant yeast
- 1 cup lukewarm water
- Vegetable oil for frying

For the Avo and Biltong Topping:

- 2 ripe avocados, mashed
- 1 cup biltong, thinly sliced or shredded
- Salt and black pepper to taste
- Fresh cilantro or parsley, chopped (for garnish)

Instructions:

Vetkoek:

    Prepare the Dough:
- In a large mixing bowl, combine the flour, sugar, and salt. In a separate small bowl, mix the instant yeast with lukewarm water and let it sit for a few minutes until it becomes frothy.

    Knead the Dough:
- Pour the yeast mixture into the dry ingredients and mix to form a dough. Knead the dough on a floured surface until it becomes smooth and elastic.

    Let it Rise:
- Place the dough back into the bowl, cover it with a clean kitchen towel, and let it rise in a warm place for about 1 hour or until it has doubled in size.

    Form Vetkoek Balls:
- After the dough has risen, punch it down, and then pinch off small portions to form golf ball-sized rounds.

    Fry Vetkoek:
- In a deep fryer or large pot, heat vegetable oil to 350°F (180°C). Carefully drop the vetkoek balls into the hot oil and fry until golden brown, turning them to ensure even cooking. Remove and drain on paper towels.

Avo and Biltong Topping:

    Prepare Avo Mash:
- In a bowl, mash the ripe avocados. Season with salt and black pepper to taste.

    Assemble:
- Slice each vetkoek in half, creating a pocket. Spread a generous amount of mashed avocado inside the pocket and stuff it with shredded or sliced biltong.

    Garnish:
- Garnish with chopped cilantro or parsley for added freshness and flavor.

    Serve:
- Serve Vetkoek with Avo and Biltong immediately while the vetkoek is still warm.

Vetkoek with Avo and Biltong is a delightful combination of textures and flavors, making it a popular choice for snacks or light meals in South Africa. Enjoy this unique and delicious treat!

Cape Malay Hertzoggies

Ingredients:

For the Pastry:

- 2 cups all-purpose flour
- 1 cup desiccated coconut
- 1 cup unsalted butter, softened
- 1/2 cup sugar
- 1 large egg
- 1 teaspoon baking powder
- Pinch of salt

For the Filling:

- 1 cup desiccated coconut
- 1 cup dried apricots, finely chopped
- 1 cup sugar
- 1/2 cup hot water
- 1 teaspoon apricot jam

For Dusting:

- Icing sugar (optional)

Instructions:

Pastry:

    Preheat Oven:
- Preheat your oven to 350°F (180°C). Grease a muffin tin.

    Prepare Pastry Dough:
- In a mixing bowl, cream together the softened butter and sugar until light and fluffy. Add the egg and mix well.

    Combine Dry Ingredients:
- In a separate bowl, sift together the flour, desiccated coconut, baking powder, and a pinch of salt.

    Mix and Chill Dough:
- Gradually add the dry ingredients to the wet ingredients, mixing until a dough forms. Chill the dough in the refrigerator for about 30 minutes.

    Form Pastry Shells:

- Take portions of the chilled dough and press them into the cups of the greased muffin tin, creating small tart shells.

Bake:
- Bake the pastry shells in the preheated oven for 15-20 minutes or until they are golden brown. Remove from the oven and let them cool.

Filling:

Prepare Coconut and Apricot Filling:
- In a saucepan, combine the desiccated coconut, chopped dried apricots, sugar, hot water, and apricot jam. Cook over medium heat, stirring continuously, until the mixture thickens and becomes sticky. This will be the filling for the Hertzoggies.

Cool Filling:
- Allow the coconut and apricot filling to cool before using it to fill the baked pastry shells.

Assembly:

Fill Pastry Shells:
- Once the pastry shells are completely cooled, spoon the cooled coconut and apricot filling into each shell.

Dust with Icing Sugar:
- Optionally, dust the tops of the Hertzoggies with icing sugar for a decorative finish.

Serve:
- Cape Malay Hertzoggies are ready to be served. Enjoy these delicious cookies with a cup of tea or coffee.

Cape Malay Hertzoggies are a classic South African treat with a unique combination of coconut and apricot flavors. They are often enjoyed during special occasions and celebrations.

Chutney Chicken

Ingredients:

- 8 bone-in, skin-on chicken thighs
- Salt and black pepper to taste
- 1 tablespoon olive oil
- 1 large onion, finely chopped
- 2 cloves garlic, minced
- 1 cup apricot or peach chutney
- 1/4 cup soy sauce
- 2 tablespoons Worcestershire sauce
- 1 tablespoon Dijon mustard
- 1 teaspoon ground ginger
- 1 teaspoon ground coriander
- 1/2 teaspoon cayenne pepper (optional, for heat)
- Fresh parsley or cilantro, chopped (for garnish)

Instructions:

Preheat Oven:
- Preheat your oven to 375°F (190°C).

Season Chicken:
- Season the chicken thighs with salt and black pepper.

Brown Chicken:
- In a large oven-safe skillet or braising pan, heat olive oil over medium-high heat. Brown the chicken thighs on both sides until golden. Remove them from the pan and set aside.

Saute Onion and Garlic:
- In the same pan, add chopped onion and sauté until softened. Add minced garlic and cook for an additional minute.

Prepare Chutney Sauce:
- Add apricot or peach chutney, soy sauce, Worcestershire sauce, Dijon mustard, ground ginger, ground coriander, and cayenne pepper (if using) to the pan. Stir to combine and let the sauce simmer for a few minutes.

Return Chicken to Pan:
- Return the browned chicken thighs to the pan, coating them in the chutney sauce.

Bake:

- Place the pan in the preheated oven and bake for 30-40 minutes or until the chicken is cooked through, and the sauce has caramelized and thickened.

Garnish and Serve:
- Once done, garnish the Chutney Chicken with chopped fresh parsley or cilantro. Serve it hot with rice, couscous, or your favorite side dish.

Enjoy:
- Chutney Chicken is ready to be enjoyed, delivering a perfect balance of sweet and savory flavors.

Chutney Chicken is a popular dish in South Africa, and its deliciously glazed and tender chicken makes it a favorite for family dinners or special occasions.

Pumpkin Fritters

Ingredients:

- 2 cups cooked and mashed pumpkin
- 1 cup all-purpose flour
- 2 tablespoons sugar
- 1 teaspoon baking powder
- 1/2 teaspoon ground cinnamon
- 1/4 teaspoon ground nutmeg
- 1/4 teaspoon salt
- 2 large eggs
- 1 teaspoon vanilla extract
- Vegetable oil for frying
- Powdered sugar (optional, for dusting)

Instructions:

Prepare Pumpkin:
- Cook and mash the pumpkin until smooth. Allow it to cool.

Dry Ingredients:
- In a large bowl, combine the all-purpose flour, sugar, baking powder, ground cinnamon, ground nutmeg, and salt. Mix well.

Wet Ingredients:
- In a separate bowl, whisk together the cooled mashed pumpkin, eggs, and vanilla extract.

Combine Mixtures:
- Add the wet ingredients to the dry ingredients and stir until just combined. Do not overmix; the batter should be lumpy.

Heat Oil:
- In a deep skillet or frying pan, heat vegetable oil over medium heat.

Fry the Fritters:
- Once the oil is hot, drop spoonfuls of the batter into the hot oil, creating small fritters. Fry until golden brown on both sides, turning them as needed. Ensure the fritters are cooked through by testing with a toothpick; it should come out clean.

Drain Excess Oil:
- Remove the pumpkin fritters from the oil and place them on a plate lined with paper towels to drain any excess oil.

Dust with Powdered Sugar:

- Optionally, dust the pumpkin fritters with powdered sugar for a sweet finish.

Serve Warm:
- Pumpkin fritters are best served warm. Enjoy them as is or with a dollop of whipped cream or a sprinkle of cinnamon.

Pumpkin fritters are a wonderful way to enjoy the natural sweetness of pumpkin in a delightful fried form. They make a great snack or dessert, especially during fall when pumpkins are in season.

Rooibos and Honey Glazed Chicken Wings

Ingredients:

For the Chicken Wings:

- 2 lbs (about 1 kg) chicken wings, split at joints, tips discarded
- Salt and black pepper to taste
- 1 teaspoon paprika
- 1 teaspoon garlic powder
- 1 teaspoon onion powder
- Vegetable oil for baking

For the Rooibos and Honey Glaze:

- 2 cups strong brewed rooibos tea, cooled
- 1/2 cup honey
- 1/4 cup soy sauce
- 2 tablespoons apple cider vinegar
- 1 tablespoon grated fresh ginger
- 2 cloves garlic, minced
- 1 teaspoon dried thyme (or 1 tablespoon fresh thyme leaves)
- 1 teaspoon red pepper flakes (adjust to taste)
- Salt and black pepper to taste
- Sesame seeds and chopped green onions for garnish (optional)

Instructions:

For the Chicken Wings:

Preheat Oven:
- Preheat your oven to 400°F (200°C). Line a baking sheet with parchment paper.

Season Chicken Wings:
- In a large bowl, season the chicken wings with salt, black pepper, paprika, garlic powder, and onion powder. Toss to coat the wings evenly.

Bake Wings:
- Place the seasoned chicken wings on the prepared baking sheet. Drizzle or brush with a little vegetable oil. Bake in the preheated oven for 40-45 minutes or until the wings are golden and crispy.

For the Rooibos and Honey Glaze:

- Brew Rooibos Tea:
  - Prepare a strong cup of rooibos tea and let it cool.
- Make Glaze:
  - In a saucepan, combine the brewed rooibos tea, honey, soy sauce, apple cider vinegar, grated ginger, minced garlic, dried thyme, red pepper flakes, salt, and black pepper. Bring the mixture to a simmer over medium heat.
- Reduce and Thicken:
  - Allow the glaze to simmer and reduce for about 15-20 minutes, or until it thickens to a syrupy consistency. Stir occasionally to prevent burning.
- Glaze Wings:
  - Once the chicken wings are cooked, transfer them to a large bowl. Pour the rooibos and honey glaze over the wings, tossing them to coat evenly.
- Serve:
  - Arrange the glazed chicken wings on a serving platter. Optionally, sprinkle with sesame seeds and chopped green onions for garnish.
- Enjoy:
  - Rooibos and Honey Glazed Chicken Wings are ready to be enjoyed. Serve them as an appetizer or as a flavorful snack.

These wings offer a unique and delicious flavor profile, combining the earthy notes of rooibos tea with the sweetness of honey for a memorable culinary experience.